Search, renew or reserve
www.buckinghamshire.gov.uk/libraries

24 hour renewal line
0303 123 0035

Library enquiries
01296 382415

Buckinghamshire Libraries and Culture
#loveyourlibrary

@BucksLibraries

LOTS OF THINGS TO KNOW ABOUT SPACE

Laura Cowan

Illustrated by
Alyssa Gonzalez

Designed by
Emily Barden

With expert advice from the UK Space Agency,
and astronomer Nick Howes

USBORNE QUICKLINKS

For links to websites where you can watch videos,
try quizzes and find even more facts about space, go to
usborne.com/Quicklinks and type in the title of this book.

Please follow the internet safety guidelines at
Usborne Quicklinks. Children should be supervised online.

Did you know it takes
about three days to fly to
the Moon in a rocket?

WOWEE! Um, but what
exactly IS a moon?

This book will explain things as
you go along. But if you go to page 62,
you'll find lots of useful words explained
in one place. And there's an index on
pages 63-64 to help you find the
things you want to read about.

The Sun is a star

That's right — a bright, shining **star**, just like the ones you see at night.

It's big and round and hot, just like all stars.

How does it make so much light!?

It's made of hot, HOT gases burning at millions of degrees. It's so enormous, over a million Earths would fit inside!

At over **four billion** years old, the Sun seems old to us, but that's not old for a star. It will keep shining for four billion more.

3

If aliens sent us a postcard...

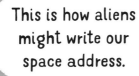

This is how aliens might write our space address.

USBORNE,
LONDON,
PLANET EARTH,
THE SOLAR SYSTEM,
THE MILKY WAY,
THE UNIVERSE

UNIVERSAL POST

Rocketmail

We live in space on a massive ball of rock and metal called **Planet Earth**.

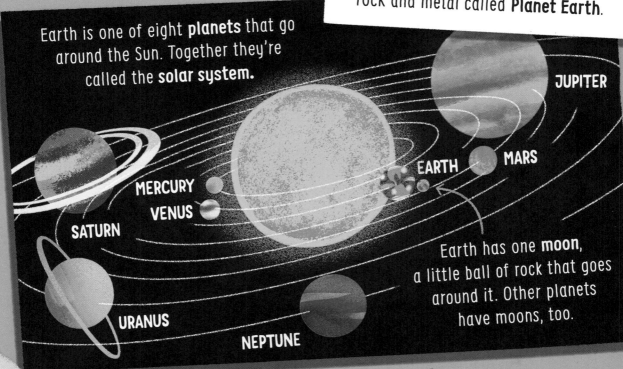

Earth is one of eight **planets** that go around the Sun. Together they're called the **solar system.**

JUPITER

MERCURY

VENUS

EARTH

MARS

SATURN

URANUS

NEPTUNE

Earth has one **moon**, a little ball of rock that goes around it. Other planets have moons, too.

The Sun is one of millions and millions of **stars** spinning together in a group called the **Milky Way**.

Lots of stars have their own planets, too.

This large group of stars is called a **galaxy**. There are lots and lots of other galaxies in outer space.

The Milky Way and all the other galaxies, as well as absolutely everything else, make up the **universe**. There's a **lot** out there.

Could there be other worlds like ours?

Dear Earthlings,

We really enjoyed our trip to Planet Earth. Thank you for having us and do pay us a visit if you're ever in our galaxy.

Love from your alien friends

Numbering the stars

It's impossible to count every single star in the universe. But **astronomers**, scientists who study the stars, have a pretty good idea how many there are. Here's how they worked it out...

First they counted each point of light in the Milky Way and found **100 billion**.

Next, astronomers worked out how many galaxies are in the universe. They did this by taking very detailed photos of parts of the sky and counting the galaxies they found.

Then they multiplied the number of galaxies by the number of photos they would need to see the whole sky. That made **200 billion** galaxies in the universe!

If each galaxy has around 100 billion stars, that means there are around **200 billion trillion** or **200,000,000,000,000,000,000,000** stars in the universe.

How stars glow

Stars give out different colours of light. The brightest and hottest are blue. Astronomers label each colour of star with a different letter.

O B A F G K M

Our Sun is a **G-type** star.

Earth's next nearest star, Proxima Centauri, is an **M-type** star.

O-type stars are very rare — there are only **20,000** in the whole of the Milky Way!

That's a LOT of stars!

If you look up at the sky on a clear night away from city lights, you might count around **2,500** stars — even without a telescope!

7

Not all astronauts were HUMAN...

Fe, Fi, Fo, Fum and **Phooey** orbited the Moon 75 times in 1972 with American astronaut, **Ronald Evans**.

ORBIT means to go around something.

SQUEAK!

Fe, Fi, Fo, Fum and Phooey weren't human astronauts — they were **little pocket mice**.

These mice were some of the last living things, including humans, to visit the Moon. But lots of animals have been into space...

Early spacecraft were too small for humans, so scientists sent animals into space instead.

Rats

The first astronauts were **fruit flies**, in 1947.

Guinea pigs

Rabbits

In 1970, the American space agency, **NASA**, sent two **frogs** into space in the **Orbiting Frog Otolith** spacecraft.

Many early astronauts were **dogs**. Scientists trained them to use simple controls in the spacecraft.

Tortoises

32 **monkeys** and **apes** have been to space...

...and an **astrochimp** named **Ham**.

How rain falls on other planets

When rain falls on the Earth, the raindrops are made of water. Other planets don't have much water — or any at all — but it still rains. So, what happens?

On **Neptune**, it rains **diamonds**.

Don't visit **Venus** - it might rain **acid** there.

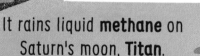

It rains liquid **methane** on Saturn's moon, **Titan**.

here's even a faraway anet where it could rain **rubies** and **sapphires**.

There's a snowman in space

Far away from Earth, past icy Neptune and Uranus...

...there's a snowman named **Arrokoth**.

It's quite big for a snowman — 33km (21 miles) from head to toe.

Scientists spotted it in the **Kuipur Belt**, a band of icy rocks at the edge of the solar system.

Is Arrokoth REALLY a snowman?

Well, it doesn't have eyes or a carrot for a nose, but it IS made of two icy balls joined together, just like a snowman!

11

Dirty snowballs with long tails

Whizzing around the solar system are dirty snowballs — giant balls of dust, frozen gases and ice that orbit the Sun — known as **comets**.

When a comet passes near the Sun, it starts to melt and loses a lot of its dust and gases.

The dust and gases follow it around in a huge cloud.

When comets get even closer, the Sun's energy pushes the dust and gases into long tails.

The tails can be *super* long – as long as the distance from the Earth to the Sun.

Snowball fireworks

Sometimes the dust left behind by a comet hits the gases that surround the Earth...

Down on the planet, we can sometimes see a kind of firework display in the sky. This is called a **meteor shower**.

Amazing!

A story of looking and learning

There are eight planets in our solar system and lots more objects — but people haven't always known that...

For thousands of years, people studied the skies with only their eyes. They could see Mercury, Venus, Mars, Jupiter and Saturn.

But they only saw them as bright lights in the sky. They couldn't see the difference between planets and stars.

Then in the 1600s, a Dutch spectacle maker built the first telescope. From then on, astronomers could see those five planets up close.

Does Saturn have EARS?

No, it has RINGS - your telescope just isn't very good!

The new technology helped astronomers to find a few more planets too.

In 1781, **William Herschel** was looking for comets. He thought **Uranus** was another comet, but then he saw it orbit the Sun in a circle and realized it was actually a planet.

There was something odd about Uranus's orbit though — sometimes it was fast and sometimes slow.

In 1842, a mathematician named **Mary Somerville** wondered if another planet — and its gravity — was making Uranus speed up and slow down.

She was right! It was **Neptune**.

Johann Galle, Urbain Le Verrier and **John Couch Adams** found Neptune in 1846, each working separately. In fact, lots of astronomers had seen it before, but thought it too slow to be a planet.

But Neptune was not the end of the story...

When is a planet not a planet?

In 1930, an astronomer named **Clyde Tombaugh** spotted **Pluto**, orbiting the Sun, just past Neptune. For 70 years, Pluto was thought of as the ninth planet in the solar system.

I'm Pluto. I'm big and round – does that make me a planet?

But, in the 1980s, scientists found out that Pluto was sitting in a band of rocks – the **Kuiper Belt**. There they found more objects very much like Pluto.

Hi!

In 2006, space experts around the world got together to decide – were they **all** planets?

Good day!

Hello!

The first eight planets have all **cleared** their orbits. This means they've pushed out of their way anything in their path – by smashing it into pieces – or picked it up as a moon.

But the little planets in the Kuiper Belt haven't done this. The experts decided that none of them – including Pluto – was a real planet. Instead they called these almost-planets, **dwarf planets**.

Going up!

In the distant future, the cheapest and easiest way to get into space could be a **space elevator**...

It won't be ready for a long time, but scientists in China and Japan are working on ideas right now. What might it be like?

Step into the elevator on Earth and travel to a huge space station. From here, spaceships take you all over the solar system!

Whee!

I'm off to catch a flight to Mars.

Welcome aboard this 07:25 service to Europa.

17

It's oh so quiet up here...

There is no air in space. Without air, sound can't travel, so, however much you SHOUT in space, no one can hear you.

When a star explodes, it does it **silently**.

The **huge** engines on this rocket make a lot of noise on Earth, but **no sound** in space.

If a meteor crashes into a planet with no air, there's **no noise**.

Even if a space orchestra was playing...

...you wouldn't hear a single note.

Ahhhh, peace at last.

It's SO relaxing out here.

19

Everyday life in outer space

While you're here on Earth reading this book, there are seven astronauts living on a space station. Life up there is very different...

On Earth, if you jump up, something called **gravity** brings you down again. But that changes when astronauts leave the planet behind.

As soon as they unstrap their seatbelts, they start to float away...

In space, gravity doesn't feel the same as on Earth. Everything feels weightless, so there's no up or down.

Bleurgh, I feel queasy!

Astronauts can't sit down, or walk around the station.

To move, they push and pull themselves along with their hands.

SNORE SNORE SNORE

They sleep in special sleeping bags strapped to the wall.

A lot of their food and drink comes from pouches and tins.

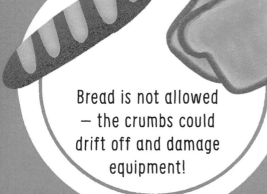

Bread is not allowed — the crumbs could drift off and damage equipment!

There are no space showers. Astronauts use wipes and soaps that don't need rinsing.

Their hair sticks out in all directions!

Astronauts have to go to the gym every day.

Because the gravity feels different, their muscles don't have to hold up their bodies in space. So they could become very weak if they didn't exercise.

How to use a space toilet

If everything feels weightless in space, how do astronauts use the toilet on a space station? It's an important question...

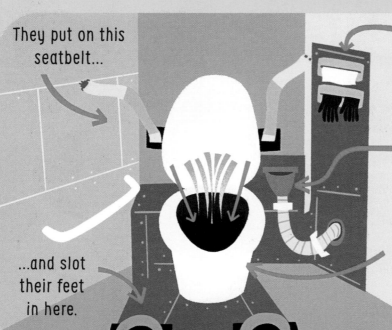

They put on this seatbelt...

...and slot their feet in here.

Here are gloves and wipes for cleaning up.

They use this funnel and hose to suck away wee.

The toilet bowl starts sucking as soon as the lid opens — poos go in here.

What happens next?

Wee is purified and turned into drinking water for the astronauts.

All poos are put in containers that zoom off into space...

PEWWW

...and burn up when they reach the Earth.

From another star system far, far away...

In 2017, an astronomer in Hawaii spotted something amazing. Tumbling past the Sun was a long, narrow, reddish object.

It was too bright to be a comet and moving way too fast to be pulled into the Sun's orbit.

Astronomers realized it was the first thing ever seen that came from outside our solar system.

They named it 'Oumuamua, (Oh-moo-ah moo-ah) which means **scout** in Hawaiian.

A few scientists think it's possible that 'Oumuamua was made by ALIENS!

REALLY?

Don't take a spaceship to Jupiter

Jupiter is **huge** — twice as big as all the other planets in the solar system put together. It's mostly made of **gases**, so it's known as a **gas giant**.

Landing a spaceship on Jupiter would be impossible, because it doesn't have a solid surface.

In fact, if you did try, your spaceship would sink.

Although the outside of Jupiter is made of gas, the inside is made of **hot**, **hot**, **hot** metal and rock.

If a spaceship sank into the middle of Jupiter, it would be **crushed** and **melted**.

The planets that are mushy on the inside

At the edge of the solar system, a long way away from the Sun, are the planets Uranus and Neptune. They're mostly made of heavy gases, known as **ices**, so they're called **ice giants**.

On these extremely chilly planets, hail falls in **mushballs** — ice-covered balls of water and a chemical called **ammonia**.

Pew! Ammonia smells bad. These mushballs STINK!

Where did they all go?

There's no hard ground for the mushballs to land on, so they sink instead. This means the insides of Neptune and Uranus are full of mush!

Baby stars make baby planets...

Baby stars are born from clouds of dust and gas called **star nurseries**.

A baby star spins.

As it spins, the baby star pulls gas, dust and rock into it.

The gas makes the baby star bigger, while the dust and rock spin around it.

Over millions of years, the dust and rock bump and stick together in little clumps.

The little clumps become baby planets. More and more dust and rocks stick to them...

...and they grow bigger...

...and bigger.

Millions — or billions — of years later, they will have grown into big, round planets, all spinning around the star.

...and baby stars eat baby planets

Sometimes a baby star's pull is strong enough to attract a baby planet.

The baby star pulls it closer and closer. Until...

...the baby star **swallows** the baby planet.

Who did it first?

Since the 1960s, humans have been going into space. But who did what first?

1961

The first **human** in space was Russian **Yuri Gagarin.**

1963

The first **woman** in space was Russian **Valentina Tereshkova.** Aged 26 at the time, she's still the youngest woman ever to go into space.

1965

The first **spacewalk** was by Russian **Alexei Leonov,** who stayed outside his spacecraft for 12 minutes.

1968

The first humans ever to **see the far side of the Moon** were the members of the **Apollo 8 crew.** Apollo 8 was one of NASA's Apollo missions to put humans on the Moon.

2001

The first **space tourist** was billionaire **Dennis Tito**, who paid NASA $20,000,000 to visit the International Space Station (ISS).

2007

US astronaut **Sunita Wiliams** ran the first **marathon** in space.

1969

The first **man on the Moon** was **Neil Armstrong**, closely followed by crewmate **Buzz Aldrin**. No woman has walked on the Moon...yet!

2015

The first **espresso** in space was made using the **ISSpresso** machine and drunk by Italian astronaut **Samantha Cristoforetti**.

What a MESS!

Humans have made a big mess on our planet, and they've made one in the space **around** it, too. There's all kinds of **space junk** orbiting the Earth!

Some space junk is big, such as broken satellites and left-behind pieces of rocket.

Some is tiny, such as flecks of paint.

Everything humans leave in space near Earth is pulled into its orbit and that's where most of it stays. It will never break down.

Altogether there are already tens of thousands of large objects and over **one hundred million** small ones.

Swerve!

The **International Space Station** (or **ISS**) is a science lab in space. Since the year 2000, astronauts from all over the world have lived and worked there.

Space junk has caused problems for the ISS, because it's all moving **superfast**.

In 2016, a tiny fleck of paint slammed into a window and cracked it.

Imagine the damage a big piece could do!

The ISS has to watch out for space junk, so it can move out of the way.

Everyone should clear up after themselves!

Back on Earth, scientists are thinking up ways to collect the junk, from harpoons to magnets. But it's a really tricky problem as there's so much of it, and it moves so quickly.

How many people does it take to land on the Moon?

In July, 1969, **NASA**, the American space agency, put the first two humans on the Moon. But thousands more people worked on the Apollo missions that got them there.

Mathematicians calculated the journey to the Moon – and back again!

There weren't many computers in the 1960s. NASA mathematicians were known as 'human computers' because they worked out everything on paper and in their heads!

Technicians made equipment, such as spacesuits and backpacks, and prepared scientific experiments for the astronauts to do.

Engineers built the spacecraft.

Two astronauts landed on the Moon...

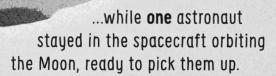

...while **one** astronaut stayed in the spacecraft orbiting the Moon, ready to pick them up.

Back on Earth, there were **20** mission controllers working in the main headquarters, Mission Control, at any one time.

Each mission controller had a team in **another** room working for **them**.

Altogether around **400,000** people worked on the mission.

One million people gathered at Cape Kennedy, Florida, USA to watch the Apollo 11 spacecraft lift off...

...and nearly **600 million** people around the world watched on their televisions.

Keeping space germ-free

Planet Earth is crawling with teeny, tiny creatures called **germs**. Some of them are good for us and some of them aren't. Either way, it's important they stay on Earth.

Lots of missions are planned to send spacecraft to other planets and moons in our solar system.

One of the things scientists are most excited about is finding signs of life.

They're not expecting to find **big** signs of life, such as alien rabbits, they're looking for **tiny** ones – germs.

In case a planet or moon does have its own germs, it's very important humans don't bring Earth ones.

EXTERMINATE!

At worst, the Earth germs could kill off all the alien ones and destroy the chance of more life growing there.

EARTH GERMS —
DO NOT
LAND HERE!

There are **International Planetary Protection laws** to stop this happening. Mars even has its own **Planetary Protection Officer**.

Sadly, I can only dream of going to Mars – my job is on Earth.

Planetary Protection laws protect the Earth, too!

PLEASE LEAVE MARTIAN GERMS ON MARS.

Only the Sun and Mercury are safe from Earth germs. They're so hot nothing could survive there.

The universe awards

Welcome to the universe awards, where the most **extreme** things in the universe are celebrated!

Size

Congratulations to **Mercury**, the **smallest** planet in the solar system...

...and to **Jupiter**, the **biggest**! Outside of the solar system, the biggest and smallest awards are all to play for as more and more planets are discovered.

BIG

HEAT

In the solar system, the surprise winner of the **hottest** planet award is **Venus**!

First I'd like to thank the Sun...

Mercury is nearer the Sun, but Venus has a thick cloud of gas and acid around it, like a blanket that keeps in all the heat.

Cold

The **coldest** planet is **Uranus**. Although it's closer to the Sun than Neptune, it has the coldest recorded temperature of any planet in the solar system — good work, Uranus!

Leaving the solar system far behind, the **coldest** thing in the universe is the **Boomerang Nebula**, a cloud of dust and gas made by a dying star.

The **hottest** thing in the universe is a **gamma ray burst**. It's a mega-hot explosion that can happen when stars blow up or collide.

The speed of light is the speed limit for the universe. NOTHING can go faster than it can.

The very special prize for the **fastest** thing in the universe goes to... **light**.

Drum roll please!

SPEED

The Sun's light is a wavy rainbow

Sunlight usually looks white, but it's actually made of lots of colours.

The Sun's light travels in waves of different lengths.

The shortest, wiggliest wavelengths look violet.

Indigo

Blue

Green

Yellow

Orange

The longest, widest look red.

The shorter wavelengths are stronger, so carry more of the Sun's heat.

When sunlight shines through rain, the water separates out the waves and you can see a rainbow.

38

Sunsets on Mars

Welcome to Mars, the **red** planet. There are **red** rocks, **red** dust and, because of all that dust, the sky is **red**, too.

In daytime, the red dust scatters the red, yellow and orange parts of the Sun's light all across the sky.

Just like Earth, the sky changes when the Sun is rising or setting.

At sunset, there's less sunlight. Only the stronger, bluer parts of the Sun's light can get through...

...which turns the sky from red to blue.

Woah! It's like the opposite of sunsets on Earth!

There's a travel network in our solar system...

It's called the **Interplanetary Transport Network**, but it's not for trains or buses. It's all to do with **gravity**.

The Earth's gravity stops you from floating away. It's what makes things fall down when you drop them.

In space, it's difficult to fly past a planet or a star without being pulled by its gravity. The bigger a star or planet is, the stronger the pull of its gravity.

Spacecraft have to use a lot of power to avoid a planet or star's gravity.

Actually, EVERYTHING has its own gravity - even us! We're just too small for our gravity to be very strong.

Neowww!

So mathematicians have worked out the easiest paths through our solar system — the ones that need the least power.

The paths use points where the gravity of two planets cancel each other out. At other points, a planet's gravity can help a spaceship to speed up or change course.

When scientists launch spacecraft to explore outer space, they send them along these paths — on the Interplanetary Transport Network.

Planet hunters

Astronomers often find new stars using telescopes, but spotting new planets isn't so easy...

Planets don't make their own light — they can only reflect light from a star. But stars are **so** bright, they hide planets in their glare.

That means it's very hard for astronomers to spot faraway planets with a telescope — even a super-strong one.

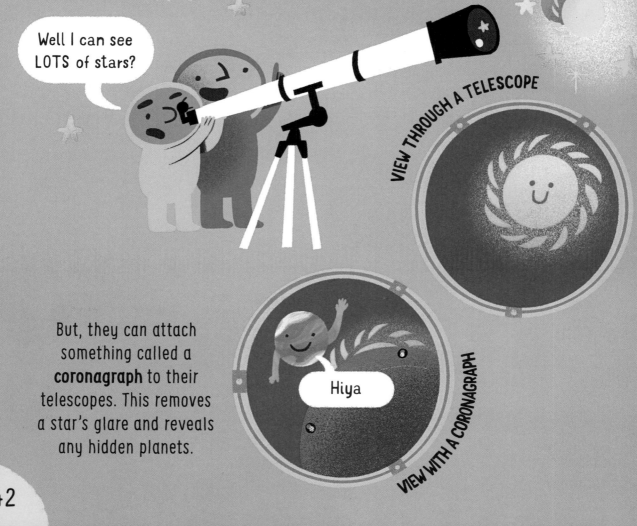

Well I can see LOTS of stars?

VIEW THROUGH A TELESCOPE

But, they can attach something called a **coronagraph** to their telescopes. This removes a star's glare and reveals any hidden planets.

Hiya

VIEW WITH A CORONAGRAPH

Planets outside the solar system are called **exoplanets**, and there are a few clues astronomers can look out for to find new ones.

Shadows
When a planet moves between the star and the person looking at it, the star's light seems to dim a little.

Wobbles
If a star wobbles and flickers, it might be because a nearby planet's gravity is throwing it off balance.

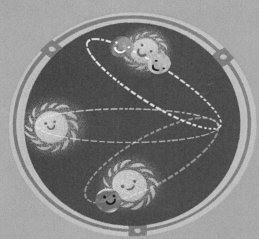

Wonky orbits
Stars travel in orbits, too — sometimes they even orbit each other. If scientists spot a star with an unbalanced orbit, it might be because the star is orbiting with lots of planets, pulling it off course.

Ocean worlds

Earth is the only planet in our solar system with liquid water on its surface. Planets and moons with lots of water are known as **ocean worlds**. Ocean worlds are especially interesting — but why?

Because, on Earth, the oceans are teeming with life.

Earthlings depend on water – even their bodies are full of it!

In fact, the oceans are where all life on Earth began!

Scientists think there could be lots more ocean worlds in our galaxy.

Who knows? Some of them could even be home to other forms of life

The secret behind a moon's wobble

The planet Saturn has over 80 moons, and even more tiny moons — called **moonlets**.

One of Saturn's moons is called **Enceladus** and it has a secret...

Astronomers noticed that Enceladus wobbles slightly as it orbits Saturn.

Wergh! Uh oh!

They realized the wobble might be caused by a hidden ocean sloshing around deep below the moon's icy surface.

It's not the only secret ocean in our solar system — many of Saturn and Jupiter's moons hide ice-covered seas.

Could there be life HERE?

Robot space adventurers

Humans haven't been to Mars yet, but they have sent intrepid robots, known as **rovers** to explore. This means whenever human adventurers do land there, they will know what to expect.

Each rover explores a different part of the planet. They study everything from weather to rocks, and send information back to Earth.

Life on Mars is hard. The rovers must work through ice, burning sunlight and dust storms.

I can collect lots of soil in my three scoops!

CURIOSITY

Inside one of the rovers is an instrument called a **CheMin**. It works out what's in the soil.

Meet **SPIRIT** and **OPPORTUNITY**, twin rovers, sent to opposite sides of Mars.

We've found rocks that show Mars used to have lakes, rivers and even a salty sea.

This rover is looking for signs that very tiny creatures, such as germs, once lived here.

Sometimes I use my MEGA laser to zap rocks.

PERSEVERANCE

Perseverance drills into the ground and fills tubes with what it finds.

Future rovers will collect the tubes and send them back to Earth in a rocket, so scientists can study what's inside.

47

How to garden on the Moon

If humans want to travel further into space, they'll need to be able to grow their own food. Plants are used to living on Earth — but can they grow in space, too?

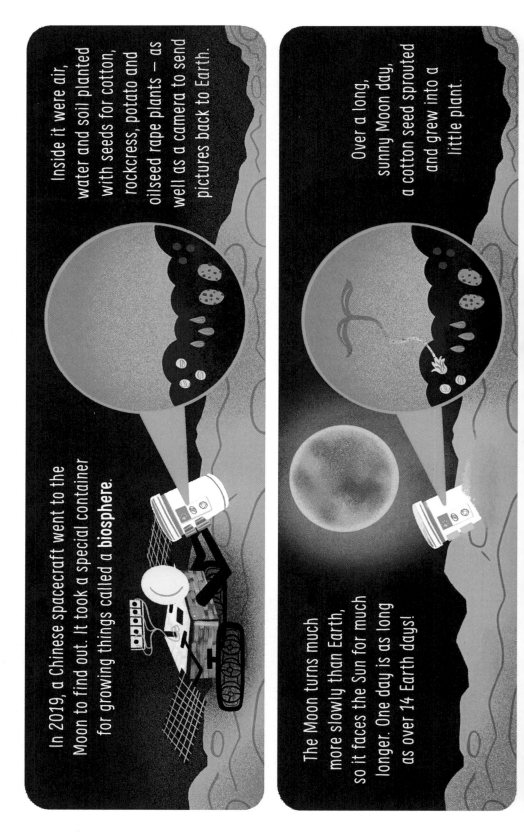

In 2019, a Chinese spacecraft went to the Moon to find out. It took a special container for growing things called a **biosphere**.

Inside it were air, water and soil planted with seeds for cotton, rockcress, potato and oilseed rape plants — as well as a camera to send pictures back to Earth.

The Moon turns much more slowly than Earth, so it faces the Sun for much longer. One day is as long as over 14 Earth days!

Over a long, sunny Moon day, a cotton seed sprouted and grew into a little plant.

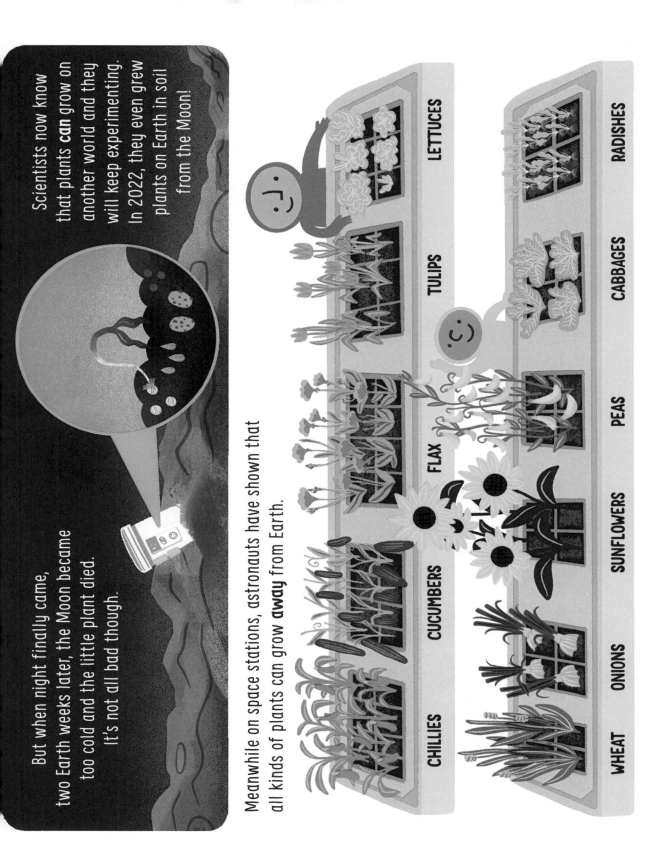

But when night finally came, two Earth weeks later, the Moon became too cold and the little plant died. It's not all bad though.

Scientists now know that plants **can** grow on another world and they will keep experimenting. In 2022, they even grew plants on Earth in soil from the Moon!

Meanwhile on space stations, astronauts have shown that all kinds of plants can grow **away** from Earth.

CHILLIES CUCUMBERS FLAX TULIPS LETTUCES

WHEAT ONIONS SUNFLOWERS PEAS CABBAGES RADISHES

Measuring the universe

Space is so big, scientists can't use the measurements they use on Earth. So to measure how far away things are outside our solar system, they use the speed of the fastest thing in the universe — **light**.

Scientists measure space by how far light travels in one Earth year. They call it a **light year**.

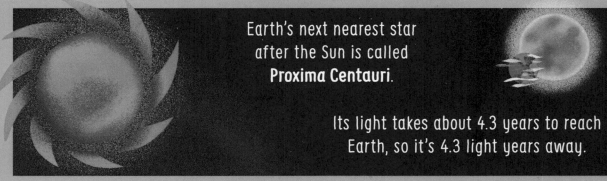

Earth's next nearest star after the Sun is called **Proxima Centauri**.

Its light takes about 4.3 years to reach Earth, so it's 4.3 light years away.

Can we drive to Proxima Centauri?

No, silly, cars don't go into space! And the journey would take over 48 MILLION years!

Even our fastest spacecraft would take about **18,500** years to get there!

Light-distant chatting

If humans ever go to Mars, there might be a hitch when they want to phone home...

Earth and Mars orbit the Sun at different speeds. This means that they are sometimes near...

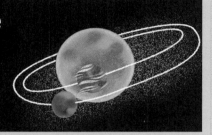

...and sometimes far away from each other.

Humans can send information — in phone calls or video chats — at the speed of light.

It takes between three and 22 minutes for light (or information) to travel from Mars to Earth...

...so conversations wouldn't be very snappy.

I'm just watching the Martian sunset. It's SO amazing... and... hello?

Yawn... um, so did you tell me what a Martian sunset looks like?

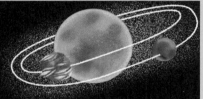

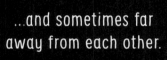

EARTH, 22 MINUTES LATER...

Moon trees

In 1971, astronaut **Stuart Roosa** took a little bag of seeds into space and flew around the Moon with them to see if being in space changed them.

There were 500 seeds from five types of tree.

So nice of you to visit!

PINE

REDWOOD

SWEETGUM

SYCAMORE

FIR

When the seeds came back to Earth, they were planted all over the world, but no one kept a record of **where**. Is there a Moon tree near you? Some of them have a little plaque!

Going to space had no affect on the seeds – Earth trees and Moon trees are exactly the same.

Colds are even worse in space

Catching a cold can make you feel pretty miserable — blocked nose, fuzzy head, itchy eyes. But in space it's even worse.

Without any gravity to drain the snot, it just sits in your nose, making you feel terrible.

And imagine what happens if an astronaut sneezes!?

In 1968, an astronaut went into space with a cold and he gave it to everyone else on the mission!

Now astronauts have to stay away from other people for around two weeks before going into space, to make sure they're not sick. This is called **quarantine**.

Set sail for the stars!

It takes lots of fuel just to go to the Moon. And there's nowhere to refuel, so how can humans ever go any deeper into space?

Well, scientists think **sailing** could be the answer. No one's made a sailing spaceship yet, but here's how one might work in the future.

Sailing ships don't need lots of fuel. The wind blows their sails and off they go!

But where's the wind in space?

Stars are made of burning gases. Some of the gases escape and blow away. This is called **stellar wind**.

When gases blow away from the Sun, they're called **solar wind**.

In the future, spaceships could be fitted with special sails so that solar wind could blow them all the way out of the solar system.

Our galaxy is bubbly

Some **massive** stars have bubbles round them.
The bubbles are made of stellar wind.

Exploding stars make bubbles, too.

Around the bubbles is
a thin, strong shell made
from gas and dust squashed
together. These bubbles
can never burst.

When bubbles squidge together, they make an enormous bubble called a **superbubble**.

Superbubbles are hundreds of light years across and full of gas.

Our solar system has been flying through a superbubble for millions of years. It's called the **Local Bubble**.

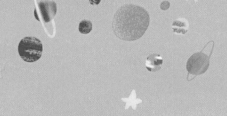

There are lots of other stars in the Local Bubble. Baby ones are forming from the gas and dust on its shell.

Telescope time machine

For hundreds of years, people have used telescopes to see faraway things.

Modern telescopes are bigger and better than ever before — and some of them have been sent into space for a better look.

On December 25th 2021, the **James Webb Space Telescope** was launched into space.

There were no astronauts aboard, so its 18 mirrors were programmed to open out on their own.

It's huge — as long as a tennis court and as tall as a three-floor building — and it can see a type of light humans can't, called **infrared**.

When light from a star travels a really, **really** long way, it becomes infrared.

Being able to see infrared means the James Webb Telescope can see far-off galaxies — and look through clouds of dust, too.

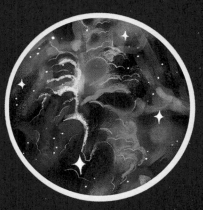

Scientists know the most distant galaxies from Earth are the very oldest. Stars here are around **13 billion** years old.

By seeing the light of these ancient stars, the James Webb Telescope is actually looking back in time — almost as far as the **beginning of the universe**.

When a star stops shining...

A star shines brightly for a very long time — for a few millon or even billion years. But one day every star will stop shining and change. What happens next?

There are all kinds of stars. But some of the biggest stars grow bigger and bigger, swallowing everything around them until...

...their insides collapse and their outsides...

...EXPLODE!!!!!

This is a **supernova**.

What's left behind is called a **neutron star**.

A neutron star is VERY tightly packed. If it were the size of a sugar cube on Earth, it would weigh as much as a mountain.

When a star becomes a hole...

Sometimes a star is so huge, at the end of its life, something different happens...

It collapses so much, it turns inside out and makes a hole in space!

It's called a **black hole**!

Wahaha help!

A black hole has stronger gravity than **anything else** in the universe. So, anything that gets too close to a black hole is pulled inside – even light.

It's impossible to **see** a black hole. But what astronomers **have** seen is glowing stars whizzing around one like water vanishing down a plug hole. In 2022, for the first time ever, they took a picture of this happening around the **supermassive** black hole in the middle of the Milky Way.

Space words

astronaut – a person who travels into space.

astronomer – a person who studies space, especially stars.

billion – a thousand million.

black hole – a hole in space with gravity so strong nothing can escape its pull. A **supermassive black hole** is the largest kind.

comet – a ball of frozen gas and rock that travels around the solar system.

galaxy – a huge group of billions of stars. Our galaxy is the Milky Way.

gas – a thing like air that isn't solid like rock or liquid like water.

gas giant – a huge planet made of gases.

gravity – a force that pulls things toward it. The bigger the object, the stronger its gravity.

ice giant – a huge planet made of heavy gases known as ices.

light waves, wavelength – light travels in waves. Its **wavelength** is the distance between the tallest points of each wave.

light year – the distance light travels in a year, used for measuring space outside the solar system.

meteor shower – fireworks in the sky, usually from a comet.

moon – an object that orbits a planet, a **moonlet** is a very small one.

orbit – to go around something. Planets go around stars and their path is called an orbit, too.

planet – a large, round object that orbits the Sun – for example Earth. Planets orbiting other stars are called **exoplanets.**

rover – a kind of robot used to explore the surface of a moon or planet.

solar system, the – the Sun and all the planets – and everything else – that orbits it.

solar wind – energy from the Sun that 'blows' like wind. **Stellar wind** is the same energy from other stars.

space station – a spaceship in orbit where astronauts can live and work for a long time.

star – an enormous ball of burning gases that gives off light and heat.

star system – a star and everything that orbits it.

star nursery – a part of space where new stars form.

supernova – the huge explosion when a big star dies.

telescope – a device for seeing faraway things, such as stars, in detail.

universe, the – everything in space.

Index

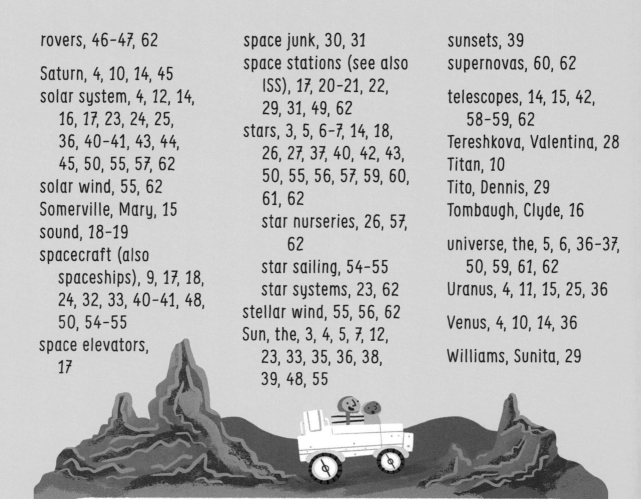

Series editor: Ruth Brocklehurst
Series designer: Stephen Moncrieff

First published in 2022 by Usborne Publishing Ltd., 83–85 Saffron Hill, London EC1N 8RT, United Kingdom. usborne.com Copyright © 2022 Usborne Publishing Ltd. The name Usborne and the Balloon logo are Trademarks of Usborne Publishing Ltd. All rights reserved. No part of this publication may be reproduced, stored in any retrievable system, or transmitted in any form or by any means, without the prior permission of the publisher. UKE.